Surviving a Media Interview
"Interview or Interrogation... Your Choice!"

By
Doc Kokol

Copyright © 2018 by Kokol and Associates, LLC

All rights reserved. This book or any portion thereof may not be reproduced or used in any manner whatsoever without the express written permission of the publisher except for the use of brief quotations in a book review.

Printed in the United States of America
ISBN-13:978-1985049321
ISBN-10:1985049325

Kokol and Associates, LLC
2107 Gibbs Drive
Tallahassee, FL 32303
www.kokolandassociates.com

Table of Contents

Introduction 1
Interviews are Opportunities 2
The Reporting Processes 2
Deadlines..3
Do your homework; the internet is your friend!.........4
YOU know what you will be asked.......................5
YOU set the interview agenda..............................5
Why did they use that quote? 6
Plain Language 6
Original 7
Message Maps 8
    Message Map Template............................9
Stop. Don't add to it 10
Put things into context..11
Bridge to key messages 12
Turn negative questions into positive messages.....14
The False Premise and Conclusion........................15
Don't speak for the other side 16
Pause to give thoughtful, positive responses..........17
Tricks and traps 17
    The Void..17
    The Seducer 17
    The Machine Gunner..............................18
    The Interrupter 18
There is no off the record 19
Cameras and Microphones are always on 19
Don't let your reporter wander 20
Parking lot ambush 20

Common sense stuff 21
Telephone Interviews..24
What to do when you say something wrong..........24
What to do when you are misquoted 24
No, but… 26
Stop talking; silence is a powerful tool....................27
Gaze into your crystal ball 28
Three strikes..28
Some final thoughts 30

Introduction

There are several, no, more than several, there are lots of books about media interviews written by reporters. This one is different, it's written by someone who makes a living as a spokesperson. I created this guide after living and teaching these skills to hundreds of public information officers, agency spokespersons and government and private sector executives. Everything I suggest that you do not do... I've done, and suffered the consequences. Learn from my mistakes and successes.

If you are looking for an academic treatise on the theory of communication, or the psychology of interviews...this is not the book for you. If you are looking for a survival guide...something to keep from having a "career-altering moment" during an interview, you have come to the right place.

This guide is built from real-world experience, working with reporters who wanted to put out a fair story and those who wanted to have my head on their wall as a trophy. Ok, if interviews are so challenging, so nerve-wracking and potentially career killers, why do them at all?

Interviews are Opportunities

There is a conversation going on about your company or agency among your employees, your customers, and the public. You must make a choice. Do you want to be a part of this conversation, or do you want others, some of whom may not have your best interests at heart, to speak for you?

This is the decision process you go through each time the media calls. Unless there is some compelling reason not to, pending layoffs, lawsuits, government secrecy rules, it's likely best to take the interview. This handbook will help you get your message out, and keep the interview from becoming an interrogation.

Reporters train to become good interviewers; you should train as well. This guide will help you learn the steps to navigate and survive a media interview.

The Reporting Processes

By the time you are contacted to do a media interview, the reporter may have already written the story, or have a good idea of how the story will play out. The reporters sole purpose for talking to you may be to guide you to a quote that fits this preconceived story. Your role is to make sure your side of the story, your key points, and your conclusions are elements of the finished story. It is a reporter's job to seek out those who disagree with you; your job is to make your position more compelling.

It's important to remember that reporters are people too. They bring different levels of experience and competence to your interview. Some have agendas and consider themselves "watchdogs," others know nothing about you or what you do, but their editor sent them to your office to do an interview.

Watchdog reporters ascribe to the theory of "Villains and Heroes." In that case, you may be the villain and a hero. In some cases, the reporter is the hero, uncovering wrongdoing and exposing sins. In that case, you may be the Villain if you don't prepare.

Other reporters want to tell a story full of color and depth. Your role, in this case, is to provide the details and context needed to make this happen. This guide will show you how.

Deadlines

A reporter's world centers around deadlines. The 6 o'clock news will air at 6, and the daily newspaper will print each day. Today's 24-hour news cycle has a voracious appetite for news, and it must regularly be fed.

When you or your staff are contacted by a reporter looking for information, ask what the deadline is. If the information is at hand and you can provide it quickly, go ahead. You don't need or want to wait until the deadline to respond. If it's going to take time to gather the information, say so, and provide a reasonable timeline. If the request is unreasonable, let them know you can't meet that deadline. I like to use the "no but" plan. I won't be able to gather the information you need by your deadline, but what I can tell you right now is...

If you want to position yourself as a reliable source of information for reporters, and there is no reason not to, make an effort to provide the information requested on time and as complete as possible. The positive aspect of being helpful to someone whose comments are read or viewed by thousands or millions is evident.

Do your homework; the internet is your friend!

Get to know your interviewer before you do the interview. Google and other search engines are a good source of information about the tone and tenor of your reporter's work. If every article published by this reporter is an investigative report on corruption or waste, it's likely you are either the target or a source.

But what about the general reporter, the person who does everything from news to puff pieces, you know, dogs with sunglasses and Halloween costume pageants. Check to see if they have reported about your industry or area of specialty. See how many sources they use, how long are the quotes. Have they become an expert in their minds about you or what you do? Most importantly, based on what you have found, what kind of questions can you expect from this reporter?

YOU know what you will be asked

If you sit down and think about your business, your agency and the issues at hand you can predict 90 percent of the questions you will be asked during an interview. Of those questions, there are likely some that fall into the category of "I hope they don't ask about this." These are the questions you need to work on first. Trust me, almost without exception at least one of these hot questions will be asked. It never fails.

Answering "how long have you been making the XYZ widget," should not take long to plan for, but answering the "when did you first learn that the XYZ widget had a flaw in it?", or "how many children have to be injured before you take the XYZ widget off the market?... well that may take a little longer.

YOU set the interview agenda

A media interview is your opportunity to tell your story. You set the interview agenda for the interview by returning to your key messages. Remember, your interview is not a casual chat, or a debate or an opportunity to educate the reporter or show just how smart you are. It is your chance to tell your story. Period. The interview process is like a choreographed dance. If you don't know the steps, you may trip and fall.

The reporter has likely gone to journalism school and learned the techniques, trick and traps needed to get you to provide them with a quote that fits their story. Together we are going to learn how to put you on equal ground and raise your chances being successful in having your information, your quote as the center of the story.

Why did they use that quote?

"Why did they use that quote... why didn't they use" ... and then they fill in the blank with the quote you wanted the reporter to use. My answer is always the same.

Why did you say it?

If you keep reinforcing your message, the key message that you want to be used, the reporter won't pick the wrong quote. It's important to stick to your key message, and I am about to show you how. Here are some tools and tips to get your key message in the story. Remember, it's all about keeping control.

Plain Language

Communication is a two-step process. You make and send the message; your audience receives and interprets the message. If you want people to understand what you are saying, use plain language. Here is an example from the Centers for Disease Control.

CDC Original Sentence: The rabies virus is transmitted through saliva or brain/nervous system tissue.

Plain language Sentence: You get rabies from germs from the spit, brain or nervous system tissue of an animal that is sick with rabies.

The standard is 8th-grade language. Avoid initials or "terms of art" that only someone in your industry would understand.

Here is one from our friends at Medicare as noted on the plain language website: www.plainlanguage.gov. Yes, there really is a Federal plain language web page.

Original

Investigators at the contractor will review the facts in your case and decide the most appropriate course of action. The first step taken with most Medicare health care providers is to re educate them about Medicare regulations and policies. If the practice continues, the contractor may conduct special audits of the provider's medical records. Often, the contractor recovers overpayments to health care providers this way. If there is sufficient evidence to show that the provider is consistently violating Medicare policies, the contractor will document the violations and ask the Office of the Inspector General to prosecute the case. This can lead to expulsion from the Medicare program, civil monetary penalties, and imprisonment.

Plain Language

We will take two steps to look at this matter: We will find out if it was an error or fraud. We will let you know the result.

Message Maps

Message maps are your safe harbor, that place that keeps you from wandering into uncharted waters, and keeps you from setting your hair on fire! The message map process I use was created by Dr. Vincent Covello. His work is all over the internet, and a quick search will show you hours of presentations he has made to public and private sector groups. The message map template shown in this guide is published with his permission. Here is a link to his web page: www.centerforriskcommunication.org. It's worth the time. Message maps have saved me grief and kept me employed as a spokesperson. Thank you, Vince.

The message maps come from research that looked at high profile press conferences, and the quotes that were used by the media. What was said, how it was said and did the media use it.

In addition, peer-reviewed research in communications shows that when stressed, people receive, process and react to messages differently than when things are calm.

The result of this study was the 3/9/27 formula. Three key points that can be spoken in 9 seconds, or 27 words, total.
Below is an example of a message map that I have used.

Message Map Template
How can the neighborhood avoid bear conflicts?

Key Message 1	Key Message 2	Key Message 3
Remove all food and trash from outside	If possible get bear-resistant trash cans	Work with your neighbors. Each home must do its part.
Supporting Fact 1-1	Supporting Fact 2-1	Supporting Fact 3-1
Trash is the most common item that attracts bears to your neighborhood	Put garbage out on pickup day, not the night before	Bears don't know property lines.
Supporting Fact 1-2	Supporting Fact 2-2	Supporting Fact 3-2
This is the time of the year bears are on the move	Clean grills and remove wildlife feeders	It's all about calories. Trash is "easy food" for a bear
Supporting Fact 1-3	Supporting Fact 2-3	Supporting Fact 3-3
Bears will just move through neighborhoods that don't have easy food.	Feed your pets inside	Removing easy food will send the bears back to natural food sources

If asked or if your key message is "How can neighborhoods avoid bear conflicts?", your answer is the top row left to right. Like this…" It's important to remove all food and trash from outside, get bear-resistant trash cans and work with your neighbors. Each home must do its part."

That's it. That's the quote you want.

Stop. Don't add to it

If you have more time, you can use the supporting facts which read top to bottom. "You know trash is the most common item that attracts bears to your neighborhood and this is the time of the year bears are on the move. Bears will just move through neighborhoods that don't have easy food. You can use supporting facts 2 and 3 if you have the opportunity.

This seems so simple, and it really is. The challenge is to focus your message. No extra words, no embellishments. Just the words you want on air or in print.

You will need more than one message map for an event, but this shows you the process. Sit with your subject matter experts, put a template up on the board, list the questions you know will be asked, and the ones you hope won't come up and build a map for each. Message maps are also great tools for prepping others if someone else is going in front of the media.

So, identify your audience, decide what questions they may have and build your message maps accordingly.

Do it now, during the calm. Have the maps reviewed, and test them.

Testing doesn't mean giving the map to your colleague and asking, "so what do you think?" Find the right audience and present your message to them. Use probing questions to see if the message you are sending is what the audience is hearing, and retaining.

Here is the routine.
- Identify the stakeholders
- List their questions
- Edit list down to most frequent questions
- Write overarching message (key messages)
- Write supporting facts
- Test the message map
- Plan for the delivery of the message

Put things into context

Paint a visual image with your words. It's important to put things into context so the reader or viewer will understand the subtleties. Try this.

Imagine a room with 1 million basketballs in it.

Now imagine a room with 3 million basketballs in it.

You can't do it, but, by providing clues, you can make this work. Like this.

"The oil spill poured nearly 20,000 gallons of fuel into the wetlands."

Ok now try this,

"The oil spill poured nearly 20,000 gallons of fuel, about as much as it takes to fill a backyard swimming pool, into the wetlands."

See the difference. Advertisers use this all the time. "Our tires run so long you could travel around the world twice before you need to change them." You don't know how far that is, but you know it a long way. Or "laid end to end we produce more than 25 miles of string cheese a day". Think visual when you create your messaging.

Bridge to key messages

Bridging is your tool to keep an interview from becoming an interrogation. Here is a key point to remember....

No One Hears the Question....They Only Hear Your Answer.

You will be asked several questions during an interview; it is very unlikely the questions you are asked will be heard or read by the audience. The reporter will use your answers and blend them into the storyline. This is important. It allows us to use bridging responses to highlight our main message and to avoid answering questions that lead down paths we don't want to go. This is YOUR interview; you are in charge unless you give it up to the reporter. Maintaining control should be subtle but direct.

Here are some typical bridging messages to help stay on message:
- What I am really here to talk about is....
- Before we get off that....
- That is not part of my area of expertise, but I can tell you...
- Let me put this in perspective...
- What I really want to talk to you about is....
- The most important point is....

I find that I use the last one, "The most important point is..." more than any other bridging statements.

Here is some behind the scenes information. Most of the time, the television reporter who is interviewing you, will not be the person who edits the package for air. The on-air product is built by an editor. The reporter will give the editor notes, or sit in the editing session.

Many editors will fast forward through the raw field footage to see what material they have. The images speed by, but the sound is still understandable. When an editor hears, "the most important point is," often they will stop and look at that take. It's just human nature. Will this guarantee that they use your quote... no... but it doesn't hurt.

Bridging can't be robotic, or the reporter just might show your audience how you are trying to avoid answering hard questions.... one of the few times they may hear the questions. Used logically, it helps you maintain control.

Turn negative questions into positive messages

Never repeat negative language. Let me say that again. Never repeat negative language. Here is an example:

> Reporter: Isn't it true that the President hasn't given you the resources you need to manage this crisis?
>
> Your response: No, it's not true that the President hasn't given us the resources we need.
>
> Edited for Air: The President hasn't given us the resources we need.

Remembering that no one hears the question, maybe this would be a better answer.

"The President is monitoring the situation closely and is committed to providing our team the resources we need to manage this event effectively." or "We are working closely with our partners and stakeholders to ensure we have the resources we need to respond to this event."

The False Premise and Conclusion

You may get a question that is not only negative but false. As Barney Fife would say "Nip it in the bud!"

Something like:

Q: When are you going to make your product safe?

A: Our product has always been safe. Then bridge to your main message.

But what if the question is false to its core?

This is the time to say:

I disagree with what you just said… then say what is correct. Or "That's just not accurate…" don't pick a fight, you can't win with someone who buys ink by the barrel or tape by the truckload. Be nice, but firm… and then move on to your main statement… again.

Don't speak for the other side

Your job in this interview is to tell YOUR story. Don't speak for the other side.

Imagine you are an executive for a coal-fired power company. You're asked about solar power, and you answer, "Well I know that the solar industry says they are cleaner and more sustainable, but we have significantly changed how we handle coal to minimize the health and environmental effects."

Can you imagine what the follow-up questions from the reporter will be? Tell your side of the story, I assure you the reporter will seek out quotes from your opposition. Remember that's his or her job; to show both sides of the story or issue.

Pause to give thoughtful, positive responses

One of the most valuable skills in an interview is to listen…. really listen to the question. It's easy to fall into the trap of hearing the first part of the question, and then start to formulate your answer, but not really listen to the whole question first.

Instead of trying to look good and fire your answer right back to the reporter, listen first and then take a second to form your answer. If it's a TV or radio interview, the pause will be edited out. If it's for a newspaper, well the reporter isn't writing "pause … pause…" in his notes. Remember I said to take a second... a pause... don't zone out and give the reporter concern if you are OK or not.

Avoid using statements like "Well that's a very good question," or I'm glad you asked me that... to stall for time to think. Just pause, think about what you are asked and answer it in a clear and concise manner.

Tricks and traps

The Void

Silence is one of the most powerful interview techniques. You answer a question, and the interviewer just looks at you...with the microphone pointed at your face... it's uncomfortable, and if you are not ready for this interrogation technique, you will fill the void, just to end the awkward pause. This is when you go off message and get into trouble. Don't do it. Give it a moment and if the reporter is still staring at you, nodding yes and smiling...just bridge to your positive main message...or ask if there is anything else.

The Seducer

This is when the reporter becomes your best friend. You like what you hear, you become overconfident and change from interview mode to "chat" mode. I'm not suggesting that you be rude, not yet at least, but when the pre-interview conversation is all about how wonderful you are, and how very smart and successful you are...standby...you are about to be had.

So be friendly right back, but stay on message, and wait for the reporter to turn hostile or aggressive. If it doesn't happen, well great...if it does, you are prepared.

The Machine Gunner

Some interviewers will pepper you with a long string of questions and then wait for you to answer them all. This technique can be very aggressive and tend to put you off your key points. Don't let it. Take a breath, compose yourself and try something like this. "I'll be happy to answer your questions but let's do them one at a time"... then bridge to your key message. Remember it's your interview, and you can set the pace.

The Interrupter

If you watch television news talk shows you know what this looks like. You are trying to answer a question, and the interviewer is aggressively interrupting what you are saying and sends you down another trail. This can be a very frustrating situation if you forget it's your interview. This is one time when turning the tables on the interviewer may be helpful. The next time you are interrupted, take a pause... longer than normal. Then start with "let me start again" and do just that. If you are on live television or radio, the pause will seem to take forever, but it just may stop the interruptions. Don't try to shout over the interruptions...that's the reaction they are hoping for. Stay calm, and bridge to your key message.

There is no off the record

This is one of those "career-altering moments I spoke about. There is no off the record. If you don't want what you said to end up as a headline, don't say it.

Most reporters don't like "off the record" statements because it's usually the good stuff and they want to use it. Don't get caught up in the semantic dance either. Off the record, not for attribution, background only can mean different thing to different people. The terms can also mean different things if said in Washington, D.C. or Tempe Arizona. Please remember, "What I just said is off the record" does not work either. There are no take backs.

If you decide to go off the record, after all these warnings, make sure you discuss just what that means to the reporter you are talking to and his or her editor.

Cameras and Mircophones are always on

This is just common sense. If you act like the camera and mic is always on, you won't get caught having one of those really embarrassing moments when you whisper something that the whole world hears. The fact that the red light isn't on the camera does not mean it's not recording. The camera may be on while you are showing the crew where they can setup. When they clip a microphone to your clothes its live… always… even if you go to the powder room.

Really, its happened. The camera and microphone are always on.

Don't let your reporter wander

I always meet the reporter and crew in the company parking lot. I escort them thought security to the interview location. I stay in the room during the interview, and I escort the crew back to their vehicle. Imagine if you will, the interview is over, it went well, and the crew is packing up. You have other things to do, so you say goodbye and go on to your next meeting. While leaving the building, the reporter stops at some employees' desks and "chats" about the topic of the interview. Can you see a problem with this? Escort them in and out of your building and wave goodbye as they drive out of the parking lot.

Parking lot ambush

Speaking about parking lots, what do you do when you are the victim of the dreaded ambush interview? First, let's discuss why this happened. It is very likely that you or your team has been contacted by this reporter or his outlet before, several times. There are some reporters who like to use the ambush technique, but they are few and far between. In most cases, you have been avoiding returning calls and email... hoping it will all go away. Surprise... it didn't.

Here is what I recommend. Stop, look directly into the camera, not the reporter and say "This is a very important issue, and your audience deserves more than us standing in a parking lot. I'll be happy to help you, but we need to set an appointment so I can give your questions the attention they deserve. How does 2:00 today work for you?"

Likely the reporter will persist. Just repeat the statement that you will help them but not in a parking lot. Be nice, stay calm. Some communications people recommend not turning your back to the camera, so they don't have the standard "walking away" footage. I think that's too awkward. The reporter and crew may follow you as you walk to your car or business. Walk don't run, don't put your hand in front of the camera lens, don't cover your face. Stay calm, be friendly, do not let them have the anger or fear shot they are looking for. Just go about your business.

As you are walking away, remember that this did not have to happen. Respond to the calls or emails.

Common sense stuff

- Silence your phone, remove ID badges and lanyards, and take off your sunglasses if possible
- Be aware of facial expressions and hand gestures
- Maintain eye contact with the reporter, not a "make my day" kind of stare, be friendly
- Keep your stance open and relaxed
- No big noisy jewelry

- No checks, herringbone or wild patterns, solid colors are good but avoid the black and white business suit look.
- Sit still. If you are in a chair that rocks or swivels try to sit still.
- If the interview is in your office, don't get too comfortable. Leaning back in your chair, and chilling is not the image you want to present.

Telephone Interviews

Almost all radio interviews and a considerable number of print interviews will be done on the phone. It's easy to forget that you are not having a conversation or "chat" with the reporter on the other end of the phone line… it's a media interview and requires all the prep and strategy as a face to face meeting does. Here are some tips to make it successful.

You can invite your subject matter expert or anyone else you want input from to be in the room during your interview. You should have your notes organized so you can find information without delay, and while it's common sense, you need to plan so that you are not disturbed. Turn off your cell phone ringer, put a do not disturb sign on your door, and take a few minutes to calm yourself.

See if you can call the reporter, rather than sit and wait for the phone to ring. Most of the time the reporter will want to call you when the equipment at the station is available and ready, but it can be nerve-wracking to sit and stare at the phone waiting for the call.

Most print reporters will be typing as you talk to them and you will be able to hear the keyboard noise. You can expect the radio reporter to tell you that you are being recorded, or that you are going to be on air live. Or at least that's what is supposed to happen.

I once answered my desk phone to hear "Hey Doc. this is "Bill" from XXXX radio station. Do you have a few minutes to talk about pandemic flu? What Bill forgot to tell me was that we were live on the air when I picked up the phone. It took me a few minutes to catch on that "Bill" was a shock jock doing a morning drive comedy show. That was my last interview with "Bill." When I got off the phone, I called his station manager…we chatted about ethics and state and federal statutes and her choice of on-air talent for a bit.

You will not be able to use a speaker phone for a radio interview. They need better sound quality than your speaker phone provides and would prefer a landline over a cell phone.

Just because you are on a handset doesn't mean you can't get help from your colleagues in the room. Most of the time, when someone knows the subject matter and can hear your side of the conversation, they can figure out where you are going…and you can write and read notes during the interview. If you are well prepared, usually the notes from your colleagues are to remind you to highlight a key point.

Last tips. Stand up when you do the interview. I know it sounds strange, but your voice is much fuller when you are standing... really it is. Other media coaches say to smile during the call...I'm not that touchy-feely. Just standing will be enough. And don't forget to turn off your radio if you have one in the room.

What to do when you say something wrong

If you do enough interviews, everyone has that moment when you hear what your mouth is saying... and your brain is yelling at you to stop! The saying "you can't dig your way out of a hole" is very appropriate here. Just stop. Tell the reporter you made a mistake and start your quote again. Don't make a big deal about it, just "I'm sorry; I didn't say that well... let me do that again", will usually work.

What to do when you are misquoted

Being misquoted, and having the reporter print or air something you said that you don't like are two different things. As we discussed earlier if you don't like the quote the reporter chose, why did you give them a choice? Build your message maps and stick to your talking points. Being misquoted is different from a factual error in the story. Each takes a different strategy.

First, take a deep breath and decide if the misquote

or factual error is important or not. If it's minor, does not set your hair on fire and won't alter your career, consider letting it go. If this is the case, just be more careful the next time you sit with this reporter. But if it's really making you crazy, here are some strategies you can employ.

If there is a factual error in the story, call the reporter and let him or her know about the error. Make sure you can defend your position. It's important to have the digital archive copy of the story changed to correct the factual error. A retraction buried below the car sales page may make you feel better but doesn't really help. Here's why.

Media outlets of any size also publish a website. The error can be changed quickly on the web to keep more readers from being misinformed. Second, getting the archive copy fixed will keep the error from winding its way through the internet... forever. As we discussed earlier, internet search engines are great resources to learn about the reporter who is going to interview you... and it's often the first place a reporter will go to get background information about you and your company or agency. Changing the digital copy will keep the next reporter from repeating the inaccurate information.

Being misquoted is more challenging. If you really are misquoted, reach out to the reporter and let him or her know that their quote is inaccurate and you want it fixed. Once again, you are asking for the story to be corrected in the archive and on their digital platforms. If it is a serious enough error, ask for a follow-up story that will clear up the mistake. You may need to escalate your request to the editor or news director. It's hard to be misquoted on television or radio unless you are the victim of unethical editing.

There are circumstances where your confidence level of the reporter or the outlet may be low, but you need to do the interview. One strategy is to tell the reporter that you will respond to their questions in writing, or provide a written statement. They hate that. Or let the reporter know that you plan to audiotape the interview. It certainly puts you in an advisory position, but it may keep the final product in the realm of reality. I don't recommend doing this on a regular basis as it does send a message to the reporter that you don't trust his or her ethics. I've done hundreds of interviews, some on very controversial topics and I've only been misquoted once that really mattered.

No, but...

Remember this phrase... no, but. It can help you get through the most difficult interview. Use this when you can't or don't want to answer the reporter's question, but you don't want to leave them without something. It goes like this.

Sue the reporter: Can you tell me if Dr. Smith is being investigated for malpractice?

You: I'm sorry Sue, Florida law won't let me discuss that, but what I can tell you is that we take any case of malpractice seriously and hope the public will reach out to us if they have any concerns about their medical practitioner.

No... but, it's a powerful bridge to help you get out the information you want the public to know.

Stop talking; silence is a powerful tool

One of the most powerful tools a reporter or interrogator has is the power of silence. You are asked a question, you answer it, and the reporter just keeps looking at you…and looking at you. Likely the microphone is pointed at you, and the reporter is smiling and nodding his or her head in a friendly manner. You become more and more uncomfortable at this awkward pause, and finally, begin to fill the void by talking. You have been had. This is when you go off topic and start saying things you really didn't plan on. It's a practiced technique, often used in small interview rooms in police stations, don't fall for it.

Answer the question, and stop. Don't say anything else. If the silence in the room become uncomfortable just ask the reporter…"Is there anything else you would like to ask me?" It's your interview, don't give up control.

You are even more susceptible to this technique on telephone interviews. The awkward pause becomes amplified if you can't get any visual clues from the reporter.

Gaze into your crystal ball

Reporters may ask you a "what if" question. They are asking you to predict what is going to happen in the future. Don't do it. Try something like this. "I don't want to speculate on what might happen, but let me tell you what we have learned from the past." Or "I can't predict the future, but what I do know is...." You know the "no... but" answer.

Also, watch out for the guarantee question "Based on what you just told me, can you guarantee that (fill in the blank). Rather than repeat negative language... No, I can't guarantee... Just move to your key point. What's important to remember is.... or "What I can guarantee is that we will continue to make every effort to see that this issue is resolved... then go on to say what you are doing.

Three strikes

Often, a reporter has already written your story or at least has a clear vision of how your story is going to fall together before you are interviewed. The goal of your interview is to get a quote from you that fits the story he or she wants. One clear indication of this is a reporter who keeps asking you the same question or the same question with slight changes. The reason you keep hearing the same question is you haven't given him or her the quote needed to fit the preconceived story.

This is where "three strikes and you're out" comes in. Once I hear the same sounding question over and over, it's time to move on. It's simple to do. "I think I have answered that question…but remember the important point is…." and go back to your key point. If that doesn't work try… "I've answered that question; do you have anything else I can help you with or are we done? Thanks for coming by."

Some final thoughts

Learning how to survive a media interview is like learning how to dance. First, you learn the individual steps, put them together in a flowing fashion and there you are... dancing, or holding your own in a media interview. You can do this.

I hope this guide was helpful, and that you will take a minute and leave a review on Kindle. Please check out my other guide on Kindle, A Survival Guide for Risk & Crisis Communication, or How to Keep Your Hair from Catching on Fire.

If you would like to know about future guides in Communication and Marketing, stop by www.kokolandassociates.com. You can always reach me at doc@kokolandassociates.com, and let me know how your interview went.

Please visit www.kokolandassociates.com and sign up for future announcements.

Please check out the companion to this book on Kindle, Crisis Communication... Don't let your hair catch on fire!

Drop me a note and let me know how your interview went at doc.kokol@kokolandassociates.com.

Made in the USA
Middletown, DE
09 June 2025